DRONES

ALIX WOOD

PowerKiDS press

NEW YORK

Published in 2016 by **Rosen Publishing**
29 East 21st Street, New York, NY 10010

Cataloging-in-Publication Data
Wood, Alix.
Drones / by Alix Wood.
p. cm. — (Today's high-tech weapons)
Includes index.
ISBN 978-1-5081-4683-4 (pbk.)
ISBN 978-1-5081-4684-1 (6-pack)
ISBN 978-1-5081-4685-8 (library binding)
1. Drone aircraft — Juvenile literature. I. Wood, Alix. II. Title.
UG1242.D7 W66 2016
623.74'69—d23

Editor: Eloise Macgregor
Designer: Alix Wood
Consultant: Mark Baker

Photo Credits: Cover © Shutterstock/Eky Studio (top), © Shutterstock/
optimarc (ctr), © Creative Commons/US Air Force (btm); 4 © DoD/
Paul Ridgeway; 5 © D Kroetsch; 6 © DoD/Dept. of Homeland Security;
7 top, 8, 14, 15, 17, 18, 22, 24 © DoD; 7 bottom © TruthDowser; 9 ©
DoD/Bobbi Zapka; 10 © US Navy; 11 © DoD/TSGT Scott Read; 12 ©
Prox Dynamics; 13 © MoD; 16 © DoD/SSGT Jocelyn M. Broussard; 19
© DoD/Senior Airman Nadine Y. Barclay; 20, 21 © Harvey Twoomey;
23 © DoD/Lt. Col. Leslie Pratt; 25 © DoD/Airman 1st Class Christian
Clausen; 26 top © DoD/Master Sgt. Shane A. Cuomo; 26 bottom ©
DoD/Gunnery Sergeant Shannon Arledge; 27 © DoD/Ted Banks; 29 ©
Blighter/Chess Dynamics

Manufactured in the United States of America

CPSIA Compliance Information: Batch #BW16PK.
For Further Information contact Rosen Publishing, New York, New York at 1-800-237-9932

CONTENTS

WHAT ARE DRONES?

A drone, also known as an unmanned aerial vehicle (UAV), is an aircraft without a pilot on board. It is controlled either by computers in the vehicle, or by a pilot on the ground using remote control. Some drones are flown using first-person view (FPV). The aircraft has a front-facing camera that sends **real-time** video to the pilot on the ground. The pilot flies the plane by looking at the video feed on a computer screen. This gives him or her the feel of sitting in the aircraft.

There are many advantages to unmanned aircraft. No human pilot is put at risk during the aircraft's mission. Also, a UAV is simpler, lighter, and cheaper than a manned aircraft. This is because it doesn't need life-support systems, or systems like ejection seats.

An MQ-9 Reaper on a training mission. There are no windows, because there is no pilot!

DRONE FACT FILE:

WHO USES DRONES?: The military uses drones for watching the enemy, and for firing **missiles** at targets. Drones are used for patrolling borders, weather forecasting, mapping, conserving wildlife, and just about anything where a view from the sky would be useful.

CAUSE FOR CONCERN: Drones can get in the way of other aircraft. Anything carrying missiles can be a cause for concern.

ACCEPTABLE?: Most people believe wartime drone missile strikes are acceptable, but as with any weapon, must only be used when absolutely necessary

Drones are being developed for a number of uses, not just military ones. In the future, a drone could follow young children around to make sure they are safe. Or a drone could be programmed to fly around your property, keeping a watch on it if you're away!

Drones like this Aeryon Scout have a "follow me" feature. This gives someone a view from above while they walk. This can be very useful during a search and rescue mission, for example.

WATCHING OVER THE WAR ZONE

A drone can act as a very useful eye in the sky over a war zone. Watching over a battle area is called combat **surveillance.** A UAV can send back information to operators on the ground. Those operators can be located on the battlefield, but they could also be thousands of miles away. The images can be used to look out for threats, and plan any attacks.

It usually takes two people to operate a military drone. A pilot takes charge of controlling its flight. A sensor operator controls the camera, and also any weapons, if the drone is armed.

This type of detailed information a drone can provide helps the military in many ways.

RQ-170 SENTINEL FACT FILE:

DRONE TYPE: The RQ-170 Sentinel UAV is a new U.S. **stealth** aircraft. That means it has a special shape which makes it very hard to detect when it is flying overhead.

TOP SECRET: Few details have been released about the RQ-170, but it is believed to be fitted with surveillance cameras

CAPTURED: In 2011 a Sentinel UAV was brought down by Iran after it was spotted flying over their territory. The U.S. claims it had been flying over Afghanistan and they lost control of it.

What the RQ-170 is believed to look like

GLOBAL HAWK

Edwards Air Force Base - April, 2001. A large jet-powered aircraft takes off from the runway. Its huge wings struggle to lift the aircraft. It is heavy as it is carrying fuel to last its long journey to an Air Force base in Australia.

Around 22 hours later, the aircraft makes a perfect landing as the sun is setting over the airfield. It had flown 8,600 miles (13,840 km) with no pilot on board! The Global Hawk RQ-4A can be **programmed** to follow a route. A pilot simply monitors the aircraft during its journey.

Global Hawk has many uses. It can take images day or night, using special **infrared** cameras. This image was taken of wildfires in California, and helped firefighters pinpoint the blazes. Global Hawk's large **satellite** communication **antenna** relays the images to people on the ground.

A Global Hawk in the air. The odd looking nose hides its large antenna.

The Global Hawk drone is a high-**altitude** UAV. It flies as high as 70,000 feet (21.3 km). It uses very powerful cameras to send back images of the areas it flies over. It can cover around 40,000 square miles (103,000 sq km) of terrain a day! It flies in a crisscross path over a target area to be sure it gets images of everything below.

While still in the air, it can be quickly rerouted to observe a new area if trouble begins somewhere else.

GLOBAL HAWK RQ-4A FACT FILE:

TYPE: High-altitude, long endurance UAV

USES: Battle management, Intelligence, surveillance, **reconnaissance**

WEAPON USES: The Global Hawk can identify and pinpoint moving targets for others to attack

USED BY: US Air Force and Navy, **NASA** and **NATO**

KILLING MACHINES

On a Sunday evening in November 2002, six **terrorists** from **al-Qaeda** were driving in an SUV in a mountainous area of Yemen. An al-Qaeda leader, Abu Ali, was in the vehicle. From nowhere, a massive explosion ripped through the silent evening. With pinpoint accuracy, the vehicle was destroyed in a direct hit which turned it into a blazing fireball. Everyone in the SUV was killed instantly.

The SUV was hit by a Hellfire missile fired from a Predator UAV. Intelligence agencies were aware that the terrorists would be in the vehicle. The Predator was able to track and hit the moving target.

HELLFIRE FACT FILE:

TYPE OF MISSILE: The Hellfire is an air-to-surface missile, which means it is fired from aircraft

WHERE DOES IT GET ITS NAME?: Originally designed for helicopters, it was called the Helicopter Launched Fire-and-Forget Missile, Hellfire for short

HOW DOES IT WORK?: Each missile is like a miniature aircraft, with its own guidance system, steering control, and **propulsion** system. Hellfires are filled with deadly high explosive.

A Hellfire missile attached to a Predator ready for a mission

Abu Ali is believed to have been involved in the bombing of the Navy destroyer USS *Cole* while it was refueling in Yemen. He is also thought to have been a former bodyguard of Osama bin Laden, and had been hunted for more than a year.

TINY SKY SPY

There are many times in a war situation when a soldier may wish he or she could safely take a peek around a corner. A new Norwegian invention, known as the Black Hornet Nano, now means that they can. This tiny UAV is equipped with a camera that can send back pictures instantly to its operator. It is perfect during the kind of missions where soldiers need to secretly find out what is going on around them.

The Norwegian and British military have been using this tiny UAV as a spy in the sky for several years. The U.S. military is now adapting it for use, too. They are adding night vision, and improving the controls to make it easier to fly. Each unit will cost around $40,000!

A Black Hornet Nano helps take a peek around a corner.

Black Hornet Nano

image display

BLACK HORNET NANO FACT FILE:

TYPE: Micro UAV

APPEARANCE: The unit only weighs the same as three sheets of paper! This model is colored to blend into a background of an Afghan village, where it has mainly been used up to now.

HOW DOES IT WORK?: It is connected to the operator using a **data link** and **GPS**. Images are displayed on a hand-held screen.

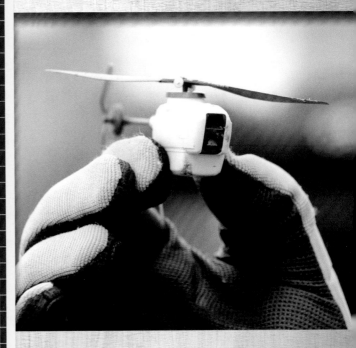

British soldiers in Afghanistan have used the Black Hornet Nano at the front line. It flies into enemy territory to record images before returning to its operator. It can fly for around 20 minutes and has very quiet electric motors. It has been used to look around corners or over obstacles, to spot hidden dangers, and to learn enemy positions.

The Black Hornet is launched from a small box that can be strapped to a belt. The box also stores the images, so if the drone is captured, the operator would not lose the information. Operators can steer the UAV or program it to fly itself.

A UAV PILOT'S DAY

After breakfast at home, you get in your car and drive to work. Your office is a shipping container on a military base. After your briefing you say a quick "Hi" to the pilot going home from the night shift. Once in the pilot's chair you have to get busy. The mission is already underway.

For eight hours you and the sensor operator take control of the UAV. Today's job is tense. You need to follow an enemy target and let the ground forces know when it will be safe to attack. You watch as the attack is successful, and then your shift ends. Thousands of miles away, you get back in your car and drive home for dinner.

A UAV pilot in his "office"

The pilot and his UAV, a RQ-7 Shadow 200

Being a UAV pilot is very different from sitting in an aircraft and flying it. Because you are not actually in the aircraft it can be a strange experience. The pilots need the same skills as traditional pilots, though. They must be fit, have good eyesight, and keep calm under pressure.

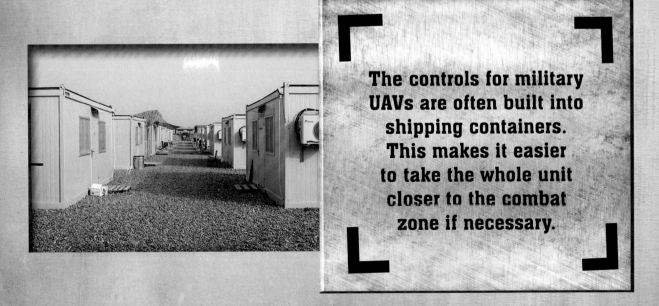

The controls for military UAVs are often built into shipping containers. This makes it easier to take the whole unit closer to the combat zone if necessary.

HUNTER IN KOSOVO

Kosovo, 1999. Hunter UAVs crisscross the skies acting as scouts, finding and filming targets for the fighter jets overhead. Because they are pilotless, the Hunters can risk flying lower than a piloted plane would dare. Hidden under some trees is a group of Serb fighters, with weapons aimed toward the sky. The Hunter sends back live video of their position. The mission is approved, and an F-16 fighter swoops in and takes out the target.

RQ-5 HUNTER FACT FILE:

TYPE: Short range reconnaissance UAV

USES: As well as military reconnaissance, Hunters have been used by **Homeland Security** for border patrols

HOW DOES IT WORK? Hunters often work in pairs. One Hunter will send images via a data link to a second Hunter, which relays them to a team on the ground.

WEAPONS: The new Hunter UAVs can now be armed with Viper Strike, a **laser-guided** bomb

During the Kosovo conflict eight Hunters were either shot down or crashed due to mechanical failure. If possible, the military likes to rescue its expensive lost equipment. This damaged Hunter has had its wings and tail removed so that it can be more easily lifted to safety.

UAVs cost a great deal of money to build. Every time a UAV is shot down it is costly. But every time an unmanned aircraft is shot down, it saves the life of the pilot who would otherwise have been flying the mission.

THE SENSOR OPERATOR

A drone's sensor operator needs to work with several different kinds of weapons and sensors. UAVs can be fitted with sensors that can detect **radiation**, and **chemical** or **biological** threats.

Drones are also fitted with video cameras, still image cameras, and infrared cameras for seeing in poor light or at night. The cameras are powerful and can even zoom in onto people's faces to see if they are a suspected target or not!

Some UAVs can be armed with weapons, and it is the sensor operator's job to program and fire them at the correct target. He or she is in constant contact with the Command Center, as they must OK any use of weapons before they can be fired.

cameras

weapons

A sensor operator locates a target during a training mission.

Laser-guided weapons such as the Hellfire missile rely on the sensor operator to guide them to their target. He or she fires a beam of laser light onto the target. The light pulses to attract the laser seekers in the nose of the Hellfire missile. Once the target is "painted" as it is called, the missile is released.

After a missile has hit the target, the sensor operator can use the cameras to check the wreckage. The images are used by the Command Center to be sure the mission was a success.

A sensor operator has so many tasks that flying the drone can seem the easiest of the jobs!

DISPOSABLE DRONES

U.S. Navy scientists have created a tiny, disposable drone that can find enemy submarines, detect tornadoes, and record conversations. Named after the cicada, an insect that suddenly appears in huge numbers, the drone is designed to work in swarms. Having so many in the sky at once would make it very difficult for the enemy to take out every drone.

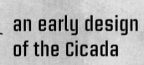

an early design of the Cicada

CICADA FACT FILE:

TYPE: Micro Air Vehicle

SPEED: 46 miles (74 km) per hour

USES: The Cicada is very quiet and looks like a bird. It can secretly listen in to conversations or vehicle movements. It can be fitted with magnetic sensors which can spot enemy submarines.

FUTURE USES: The drone cannot send back images yet but may be able to in the future

Cicadas have no propellers or engines. To get them to where they need to be, the Navy will drop them from either a balloon or a bigger drone. Navy test flights dropped the drones from 57,000 feet (17.3 km). With their targets' GPS **coordinates** programmed into them, they landed within 15 feet (4.5 m) of their targets!

The Navy's redesigned Cicada drone (below) is smaller than ever. It can fit in the palm of your hand!

Even cheaper drones are coming! Researchers have built a low-cost 3D printed disposable UAV. The drone is made up of nine plastic parts that snap together. It weighs 4.4 pounds (2 kg), and is 5 feet (1.5 m) wide. The materials for each drone cost only around $9! These drones could be used for one-way deliveries, searches, or reconnaissance missions.

A swarm of Cicadas dropped from a larger drone make their way down to the ground.

PREDATOR STRIKE

In September, 2011, in Yemen, a lone vehicle was parked by the roadside. The men had gotten out to stretch their legs and have breakfast. One of the men was Anwar al-Awlaki, a wanted al-Qaeda member. The men suddenly noticed two Predator drones heading straight toward them. They ran to the vehicle and tried to flee, but it was too late. A Hellfire missile hit the vehicle and they were killed instantly.

The Predator drones were being operated from a secret CIA base. The operators had intelligence that al-Awlaki would be in the car, and had been following it for some time. They needed to wait until the men were in an open area, so as not to injure innocent people.

Anwar al-Awlaki was an American and Yemeni religious leader. Officials believe he recruited and motivated terrorists, and planned terrorist operations for al-Qaeda.

He was the first U.S. citizen to be targeted and killed in a U.S. drone strike. In the vehicle was another American, Samir Khan, who edited al-Qaeda's website magazine.

An armed Predator

Unfortunately during conflicts innocent people do get hurt. To try to prevent this from happening, officials have a database of terrorists, listing their known crimes, locations, and contacts. Experts decide if it is possible to capture them instead, or if they must direct a drone strike. Intelligence experts and military officials update the list. Once the names are put forward, the president or the CIA director then approves the missile strike. It is not a decision to be taken lightly.

PREDATOR FACT FILE:

TYPE: Medium-altitude, long-range aircraft

VARIATIONS: The RQ-1 is a reconnaissance aircraft. The MQ-1 is a battle aircraft.

PREDATOR RQ-1 EQUIPMENT: Radar, GPS, satellite communication, video recorders, and cameras

PREDATOR MQ-1 EQUIPMENT: Hellfire missiles. The cameras are replaced with a targeting system.

REAPER MQ-9

The Reaper is similar to a Predator, but much larger. Predator drones can carry just two 20-pound Hellfire missiles. The Reaper has the ability to carry many more weapons. It can carry a combination of Hellfires and several larger 500-pound bombs.

Each huge MQ-9 aircraft can be taken apart and loaded into a container. The Air Force Special Operations Command can pack up an MQ-9 in less than eight hours, fly it anywhere in the world on a C-17 Globemaster III, and have it ready to fly in another eight hours!

A Reaper being prepared for a training mission at Creech Air Force Base, Nevada.

REAPER MQ-9 FACT FILE:

TYPE: Medium- to high-altitude, long-range aircraft

USES: Intelligence, surveillance, and reconnaissance. It can also be used to fire missiles and drop bombs in battle.

WEAPONS EQUIPMENT: The Reaper has a weapon targeting system. A laser range finder helps the operator "paint" a target for the laser-guided missiles to hit.

CAMERA EQUIPMENT: Its cameras can provide both infrared and image-intensified color images. A color nose camera provides images the pilot can use for flight control.

A Predator's Hellfires are designed to hit their target. Damage outside their target is small, as they are not that powerful. The larger bombs that a Reaper carries would destroy a much larger area.

A 500-pound GBU-12 Paveway II bomb being fitted to a Reaper

TAKEOFF AND LANDING

A drone's takeoff can be quite low-tech! Some smaller drones such as this Raven are simply thrown into the air. Other larger drones are sent into the sky using a catapult.

Large drones, such as the Predator, take off and land along a runway. They are controlled just the same as a piloted aircraft would be, except the pilot is not in the plane.

A ScanEagle UAV is launched into the air using a catapult.

It is very important to be able to retrieve a UAV. In 2012, Iran captured a U.S. ScanEagle when it flew over their airspace. By studying the captured UAV, Iran began to produce their own, based on its design.

A ScanEagle is trapped successfully in a recovery net. The net is designed not to damage the UAV.

Other ways of landing a UAV include a belly landing, or being caught using a wire and hook. Some drones have parachutes, and some can be recovered by manned aircraft. The U.S. Navy sometimes uses trained sea lions to recover drones that have fallen in the sea. A pinger on the drone sends out a signal. The sea lion finds the UAV and attaches a rope to it so it can be lifted to the surface!

DEFENDING AGAINST DRONES

How do you defend your skies against drones? Even friendly drones may fly into dangerous areas such as near busy airports. News agency drones recently hampered firefighters struggling to put out fires in California. The firefighters' helicopters had to stop operations because they might have collided with the drones.

Al-Qaeda uses several tactics to avoid drones. They **jam** the frequencies drones use for communication, or use snipers to shoot drones down. Men will hide from drones in underground shelters or in the shadows of buildings. Sometimes they burn tires to hide under the plumes of black smoke.

Drones are difficult to detect because they are smaller and lighter than regular aircraft. When radar was invented, developers made sure small objects in the sky, like birds, didn't get picked up by the radar screen. New systems have to be able to tell the difference between a bird and a drone.

AUDS FACT FILE:

TYPE: Anti-UAV Defense System

HOW DOES IT WORK?: Smart sensors detect, track, and classify any UAV. It uses radar to detect the target. Software then identifies and tracks the drone. A disruption system then jams the UAV's communications and disables the drone.

WHO MAY USE IT?: Airports, the military, VIPs, power stations, large event organizers

Other methods to stop drones in an area's air space include a high-tech solution using lasers, and a low-tech solution using nets! A handheld "net gun" has been developed that simply shoots a net into the air to entangle a small UAV.

The U.S. Navy has started using a new laser weapon system that fires an invisible laser beam that burns up the target. It can be fired by one sailor using a video game-like controller.

An anti-UAV defense system (AUDS)

GLOSSARY

al-Qaeda: A radical Sunni Muslim organization that wants the elimination of Western presence in Arab countries.

altitude: Distance of an object above a given level.

antenna: A device for sending or receiving radio waves.

biological: Relating to living things.

chemical: Relating to chemistry.

coordinates: A set of numbers used to locate a point.

data link: A link allowing transmission of data from one place to another.

GPS: A navigation system that uses satellite signals.

Homeland Security: The body that deals with terrorist threats on American soil.

infrared: Light waves that are outside of the visible part of the light range at the red end, which we can see.

jam: To make it impossible to understand information by sending out interfering signals or messages.

laser-guided: Can be guided by a laser beam to its target.

missile: A weapon that is shot.

NASA: National Aeronautics and Space Administration.

NATO: North Atlantic Treaty Organization.

programmed: Provided a computer with coded instructions to perform a task.

propulsion: Forward motion of a body produced by forces.

radiation: Energy radiated in the form of waves.

real-time: Describing the actual time an event occurs.

reconnaissance: A survey to gain information.

satellite: A body in orbit around Earth used for communication.

stealth: A design making aircraft difficult to detect by radar.

surveillance: Close watch.

terrorists: People or groups that scare or threaten with violence illegally.

FOR MORE INFORMATION

BOOKS

Collard, Sneed B. *Technology Forces: Drones and War Machines* (Freedom Forces). Vero Beach, FL: Rourke Educational Media, 2014.

Hama, Larry. *Unmanned Aerial Vehicles* (High Interest Books: High-Tech Military Weapons). Steelville, MO: San Val, 2007.

Hamilton, John. *UAVs: Unmanned Aerial Vehicles* (Xtreme Military Aircraft). Edina, MN: ABDO Group, 2012.

Scholastic. *Drones: From Insect Spy Drones to Bomber Drones*. New York, NY: Scholastic, 2014.

Due to the changing nature of Internet links, PowerKids Press has developed an online list of websites related to the subject of this book. This site is updated regularly. Please use this link to access the list:
www.powerkidslinks.com/thtw/drones

INDEX